STRENGTH
FOR YOUR
JOURNEY

21 Days to An intentionally Stronger You

Renee Dantzler, CPT

STRENGTH FOR YOUR JOURNEY
21 Days to An Intentionally Stronger You
Copyright © 2019, Renée Dantzler

Editors: Susan Green and Zachary Minton
Photo Credit: Jackie Hicks (Fond Memories Photography)
Cover Design by: SPJ Graphic Designs

Direct Requests to:
www.reneedantzler.com

ISBN – 978-0-578-55480-8

Special Thanks

First and foremost, I thank God who is the ultimate source of my strength. I cannot fathom how people get through life's challenges without Him – without hope in a higher power. Without God I am nothing but through His Son Jesus Christ, who is the head of my life and the source of my strength I am here today a stronger woman.

Heartfelt Expressions

To my loving wife,

I am honored and humbled you would ask me to write heartfelt expressions for your book. I have known you since we were teenagers and watched you go through various stages of life. I took you through hell in our marriage, yet you stayed with me and I know that you are stronger for having endured what I put you through. I watched you battle breast cancer and come out stronger after it. I have seen how you handled this latest challenge in the death of our youngest son. I saw how that took the wind out of your sails. Again and again, I see you take a punch and get knocked down, but not knocked out. This book is a blessing to all that read it because of what you have gone through.

Douglas Dantzler

Dedication

I dedicate this book to my husband Douglas, (second only to Jesus Christ) who is the wind beneath my wings. He encourages and motivates me to go out of my comfort zone to push to higher heights. Babe, thank you for your continued love, support and being a source of strength to me and our family. I am ever so thankful to God for you!

To my three sons Andre, Anthony, and Andrew who if they had not challenged me as their mother and caused me on many occasions to fall on my knees and pray, I would not be the pillar of strength I am today. Thank you for striving to be the best son's you could be. You may not be perfect, but you are perfectly mine and I love you.

Table of Contents

Introduction

As a Certified Personal Trainer, I know how important it is to be strong physically and mentally. Building strength is not as simple as walking into the gym, lifting weights and "poof!" You are strong. It takes a level of resistance and amount of time (time and tension) that the muscle is under pressure to gradually build strength. When you work muscles to the fullest potential, you feel the burn as if it a fire ignited. It also takes mental strength to withstand the tension and keep pushing the muscle to its full capacity and the belief that you can do it. This does not apply just to the gym or physical fitness, but every area of your life.

The purpose of this book is to inspire you to continue to stand strong despite resistance, life's pressure, and challenges. Some of the challenges I have faced include financial, marital, health, career change, and the death of my youngest son. Despite the challenges I continue to learn how to navigate life, stay encouraged and find strength from within to keep going.

I married my high school sweetheart just one month after graduating from high school. We were young and had no idea what we got ourselves into. Early on in our marriage, we argued all the time. Whether it was about finances, family, sex, it did not matter – we did not see eye to eye. I spent many nights crying, then going to work under stress. I was not sure if it was my insecurities but I always suspected infidelity. I never saw any real proof of infidelity, other than the fact that I saw him hanging around this woman at his job. Despite many threats and attempts to leave, the Lord always spoke to my heart not to leave – to stay strong. Leaving is easy; staying is hard and takes a strong woman stick it out in the face of adversity. I was determined to follow God's Word. This facilitated strengthening my faith in God. It was not until years later that my suspicions confirmed in marital counseling. Now in our thirty-two years of marriage, he is my best friend. We do not just love one another – we _like_ each other. We communicate well, we love, respect and honor one another. We use our marriage as a testament of strength, commitment, faith, and forgiveness. Remember, forgiveness takes strength.

When I received the breast cancer diagnosis in 2012 it came as a big surprise to me because there was no history of the disease in my family. I was (and still am) a young woman at the age of forty-two. Now a breast cancer survivor over eight years I understand the importance of physical activity and positive thinking. While I was going through radiation treatment, my oncologist would always tell me to stay positive. He was so proud of the fact that I worked out regularly and stressed how important both were to my recovery. Although there were days, I was scared, I pressed on through two lumpectomy procedures and eight weeks of daily radiation treatment. I did not have any major side effects from the surgery or treatment. The Lord has allowed me to meet other women who are going through it and I can encourage and help them to think positively, have hope and keep it moving.

After my job as a corporate trainer in 2015 ended, I did not know what to do. The news came as an overwhelming blow at first, but it was God's way of pushing me towards my destiny. I was with the organization for over 20 years. He knew that although I did not enjoy my job, I had become so complacent that I would not leave on my own. At this time, I had already started personal training on the side and loved it! The setback prepared me to do full time what I am passionate about today – personal training.

Unexpectedly losing my youngest son in a tragic drowning accident in 2016 is the most devastating thing I endure every day of my life. He was in the prime of his life. He turned 18 in May, graduated from high school in June, and passed in July. He had been accepted to attend Morgan State University that fall semester. Andrew was full of life, zeal, and energy. To know him, you had no choice, but to love him. His smile lit up the room. It still rocks my world today as I write. This does not make me less strong – this makes me human. Many people say to me, "you are strong!" Although I do not always feel strong, I believe the strength of God resides inside me to push past the pain.

Experts say it takes 21 days to form a habit. With that concept in mind, I put together this 21-day strength guide to help you get a jump start to a stronger you. Long after the 21 days have passed, I highly recommend that you continue practicing the tools provided to you in this book. Remember if you do not use the tools provided to you, you can lose it quicker than 21 days it took to establish it. This strength guide will help you tap into your inner strength for whatever your life journey, but it must become a continual process.

THE JOURNEY BEGINS

Day 1

DAY 1: Time - A Rare Commodity

Have you ever thought, or said to yourself, "I wish I had more time?" If only I had more time I would... Who has not said this at one time or another? The same 24 hours a day you had 10, 15, 20 years ago you still have today. You must treat time as a rare commodity. It is something that we cannot get back. Oh sure, people will say things like, "I can make up for some lost time," but what you are doing is wasting present time and stealing from the future that is not promised.

It is imperative to maximize each moment – while you are in the moment. The issue most people share is that we do not prioritize the amount of time we have. The day is often jam-packed with a bunch of activities that do not add value to our lives or propel us towards our goals, purpose, and destiny. I am a firm believer that we make time for the people and for the activities we want. We take for granted we can get some things done tomorrow or another day. Whoever told you that tomorrow was a guarantee told you a bald-faced lie. Tomorrow is not guaranteed. The next hour, minute or second is not either. We must redeem the time we have. Remember, time is a rare commodity, treat it as such – *value it*. Cherish the time you have with those in your life. There are 24 hours in a day, but what you do with it is totally up to you. Make the best of your time by creating a plan of action and executing.

Carpe Diem... Seize the day!

STRENGTH ACTION PLAN: Identify an area in your life you can organize to manage your time more efficiently. Make notes of your plan here:

_____

_____

_____

_____

_____

_____

_____

_____

_____

_____

_____

_____

_____

Day 2

DAY 2: Perseverance

Take a moment and think of a time when you told yourself that you did not want to complete a task. You might have something right at this moment that you have put off because the task seems just too daunting. Now ask yourself, "If I do not do it, what opportunity and ultimate goal can it affect?" No one is exempt from life challenges and trials; we all have them. Some trials and challenges are greater than others, but a challenge none the less. How you approach those challenges and emerge as a victor is totally up to you. When I experienced tough times in my marriage, (spiritually speaking it was under attack) I could have easily chosen to leave and just say, "The heck with it, I can do bad by myself." However, I chose to believe God; I chose to believe things would change for the better and that my husband would do better by me. By standing steadfast, praying, and trusting God despite what it looked like, I persevered.

My husband and I do not have a perfect marriage, but are now walking in the divine purpose of Marriage. There comes a time in all our lives when we think to ourselves, "I can't do this, or I do not want to do this." Whatever your "THIS" is, do not give up. On the other side of your

"THIS" is your answer to a prayer, an open door, and a victory. Every time you push yourself out of your comfort zone and overcome an obstacle, you become stronger.

I often hear my clients say during training sessions, "This is HARD" or "I CAN'T do that." I do not subscribe to that theory. Those are both four-letter words and prohibited during training sessions. I prefer the word "challenging." A challenge is what makes you stronger. If everything came EASY (another four-letter word) then you would never grow, improve or persevere. Perseverance is never giving up. Never giving up is how you persevere!

STRENGTH ACTION PLAN: Identify an area in your life that you can show

perseverance. Make notes of your plan here:

_____

_____

_____

_____

_____

_____

_____

_____

_____

_____

_____

_____

_____

Day 3

DAY 3: Position Yourself Properly

I used to wonder why I like to talk so much. My family often teased me because (in their opinion) I talked too much, or I had what some used to call "the gift of gab." Then I realized one day that I do like to talk and it is exactly that – a gift. So, I put that talking to good use by having conversations with God. Prayer is a powerful tool and a weapon. A posture of prayer positions you before our creator; the very one who can make a difference in our circumstances and our lives.

Have you ever tried to convince someone to do or see something from your perspective and you just could not get them to do so? On many occasions, I would try to influence my husband to do what I wanted or for him to see things my way. I do not know when I finally got the revelation and realized I was talking to the wrong person. The ONE I should have the conversation with is God. I remember the time when my husband and I did not see eye to eye about moving to another state. I was adamant about staying and he was adamant about moving. It felt as though I was talking to a brick wall. Finally, I concluded that I needed to remain in a posture of prayer for us to come to an agreement even if that meant I was not right.

After several prayers, we finally and peacefully came to an agreement that moving was in the best interest of the family.

The best position to be in to receive the best is from the best – God! Get in His presence and His will. Get in position!

STRENGTH ACTION PLAN: Identify an area in your life that you have been trying to do on your own that you can now position yourself in a posture of prayer to prepare for what God has in-store. Make notes of your plan here:

_____

_____

_____

_____

_____

_____

_____

_____

_____

_____

_____

Day 4

DAY 4: Grow Through What You Go Through

My husband and I went to a memorial/remembrance service for grieving parents. At the end of the service, they gave out bulbs to all the parents to plant in honor of our children – knowing that it is important to grieving parents such to always honor and remember a lost child in any way possible. I was not sure what type of plant it was or how long it would take to bloom.

One day I started noticing the dirt rise. Initially, it startled me to see the dirt lifting because it looked deformed and weird. A day or two later I noticed something breaking through the dirt's hard surface. The Lord dropped in my spirit, just like life is sometimes hard and things start dirty, the process to grow may look weird, but be patient you will grow into what I designed you to be.

We all will inevitably face some adversity or challenges in life. No one is exempt from going through tough times. It is how you handle those times that make the difference. You can either allow yourself to stay stuck amid a hard time or grow through what you go through. The choice is yours.

Remember the process may be hard and dirty; it may even look odd and weird, but you will break through and give birth to something beautiful! Be patient, allow yourself to grow and blossom into the beautiful person God created you to be.

"Hardships often prepare ordinary people for an extraordinary destiny..." C.S. Lewis

STRENGTH ACTION PLAN: Identify a challenging area in your life that you

can use to grow and blossom from. Make notes of your plan here:

_____

_____

_____

_____

_____

_____

_____

_____

_____

_____

_____

_____

Day 5

DAY 5: Encourage Yourself

Being the baby of my family for so long, I was used to getting a lot of attention. That carried over into my adult life. I had what is referred to as "youngest child syndrome." I was used to getting all the attention. Who does not like attention? As an adult, I constantly looked for accolades, attention, and pats on the back from other people. Well, when that did not come, I was often left disappointed and had no one to push me to keep going.

God spoke to my spirit and said to stop waiting on people and just go ahead and encourage yourself. He reminded me of David in the Bible encouraging himself in the Lord in 1st Samuel 30:6. I had to learn to tell myself, "You can do it..." "You got this..." "You are strong."

After losing my son, I lost my momentum in life and started slipping with my wellness. In the process, I put on weight and started feeling very unhappy with myself. As a personal trainer and coach, I am supposed to set an example and be a picture of health -- right? So, I started encouraging myself by re-instituting daily affirmations -- reminding myself that I am strong! Confessing, "I eat well, I live well, I am well, and all is well. I am

STRONG emotionally, physically and spiritually. I am a picture of health, I am in the best shape of my life, and I eat and live healthily. I am strong and beautiful. I can and I will lose this weight gained." "*I can do all things through Christ who strengthens me.*" (Philippians 4:13)

There comes a time in life when you *MUST* take time to motivate, inspire and encourage yourself just like David. Encourage yourself in the Lord today! It is a *MUST*!!!

STRENGTH ACTION PLAN: Identify at least 5 positive affirmations that you can speak to yourself every day. Place them on your mirror and decree and declare them to yourself every day! Make notes of your plan here:

_____

_____

_____

_____

_____

_____

_____

_____

_____

_____

_____

Day 6

DAY 6: Strength and Endurance

One of my training session with my personal trainer was all about endurance and strength. Let me tell you, I called on the name of Jesus by set number 4 and 5. I prayed God would come down himself and deliver me from this workout.

The workout consisted of the following:

- Warm-up set – 20 deep squats – bar (45 pounds)
- Set 1 – 20 Squats – 65 pounds
- Set 2 – 20 Squats – 85 pounds
- Set 3 – 20 Squats – 95 pounds
- Set 4 – 20 Squats – 105 pounds
- Set 5 – 20 Squats – 115 pounds

In between each set of squats he had me do the following exercises as an *"Active Rest"*:

- 100 triceps – pulldowns
- 30 triceps/reverse grip – pulldowns

When we returned to the squats, I tried to negotiate and barter just like we do with God. I said, "Make it heavier and I will do eight reps"... (This way I could get it over with sooner). "Look at the time, our session is over, and my legs cannot take anymore." I was trying to talk my way out of the last test – I mean set, but that was not in my trainer's master plan. It would not accomplish the end result – Endurance!

He said, "No! The session is not over until we are finished! You have one more set." With sweat pouring down my face, and some tears mixed in, I finished my final set.

Are you strong enough to endure the weight and pressures of life? I submit to you a resounding "YES" you are. *"We can do all things through Christ, who gives us strength."* (Philippians 4:13)

STRENGTH ACTION PLAN: Identify a time in your life you thought you were not strong enough to endure, yet you did. Identify something you are dealing with now and tell yourself you are also strong enough to endure this. Make note of your plan here:

_____

_____

_____

_____

_____

_____

_____

_____

_____

_____

_____

Day 7

DAY 7: Discipline Is Key

I tell my clients all the time that the journey to staying fit is not for the faint of heart. Losing weight and getting into shape for a special event is easy – maintaining it is the challenge. It requires what I call the "3 D's of Fitness": Discipline, Dedication, and Determination. These are keys to a successful fitness journey. However, without faith, they will not work. During a conversation with one of my clients I asked the question, on a scale of 1 to 10 how bad do you want to achieve your goals? My client answered, "7". I told my client that to make that a 10 she needs to apply these principles to her journey every single day. Without *dedication, determination,* and most of all *discipline* she will find it a challenge to stay the course. However, she had to have the faith that she could do it. Most people start determined to achieve their goals.

On many occasions, we are dedicated, but when motivation is lacking, (these will come and go) discipline will always be the key factor in which we have good success. You must have the faith that it is possible. You must believe that you can do anything you put your mind, body, and energy to do. The Bible declares in Hebrews 11:1, "...*faith is the substance of things hoped for, the evidence of things not seen."* You must believe it before you even see it.

Listen, it is not going to be easy. Nothing worth your time and energy ever is, but it is worth it, you are worth it. Have faith; there is nothing you cannot achieve.

STRENGTH ACTION PLAN: Identify an area in your life where your faith is not strong; determine how you can start believing positively in that area of your life. Make notes of your plan here:

_____

_____

_____

_____

_____

_____

_____

_____

_____

_____

_____

_____

Day 8

DAY 8: Practice Self-Care

Some of us are so busy helping others and taking care of everyone else that we often forget to refuel and replenish ourselves. You cannot pour from an empty cup. You cannot drive anyone anywhere on an empty tank. You only have one of you. Take care of yourself because wherever you go, there you are. You cannot get away from you!

As the safety announcements on airplanes say, "The oxygen mask drop from an overhead compartment. To start the flow of oxygen, pull the mask towards you, and place it firmly over your nose and mouth. Secure the elastic band behind your head and breathe normally. Put your oxygen mask on before assisting small children or anyone else." How are you going to help someone if you pass out?

I train women, men, teens, athletes, and seniors. I have discovered that most women tend to put so many others before themselves. We put children, spouses' parents, friends, jobs, careers and even pets first. Learn to treat yourself with love, respect, kindness, and discipline is practicing self-care and can transform your life.

Make sure YOU pray, YOU get proper rest and sleep, YOU go to a spa, YOU relax, YOU read, YOU go see a funny movie, YOU eat well, YOU enjoy a day out with friends, YOU go to a ballgame... Do what is prudent and profitable for a replenished and refilled YOU. In other words, fill your cup first. Then you can pour out from you. Self-care is necessary in to be of any use to anyone else!

STRENGTH ACTION PLAN: Identify areas of your life you can start

practicing more self-care. Make notes of your plan here:

_____

_____

_____

_____

_____

_____

_____

_____

_____

_____

_____

_____

Day 9

DAY 9: How Bad Do You Want It?

In the book of Genesis of the Bible, Chapter 18, Jacob agreed to work for Laban (his soon to be father–n-law) to be allowed to have Rachel (Laban's daughter) as his wife. After the first seven years, Laban gave him Leah who was not as beautiful as Rachel. Laban tricked him, but he wanted Rachel so badly. He agreed to work another seven years just get what he wanted. He worked for Laban a total of fourteen years (this was not the original plan).

How often have you worked hard for something and it did not happen when or how you thought it should? Do you just assume by default, that it was not supposed to happen and quit? Some of us start second-guessing ourselves, thinking, "Maybe it was not meant to be." Sometimes we talk to the wrong people who suggest that we are wasting our time. Often, we talk ourselves out of the blessing. If you want it bad enough you will stay the course. Do not get off track.

Work hard for whatever it is YOU want because it will not come to you without a fight. You must be strong and courageous and know that you can do anything you put your mind to. God will supply the resources you need. Just pray to ask Him for them. Then get your grind on! Do not quit and stop until you see your vision come to fruition. Of course, you are going to encounter speed bumps, roadblocks, setbacks and more -- but that is part of the work. It is just that now you must work around all of the speed bumps, roadblocks, and setbacks. Work hard with reckless abandon. This means that you will go after it and put your all into accomplishing your vision and goal without thought or regard to the challenges, missteps, and even failed attempts. Always keep the accomplished goal in mind.

It could be getting your degree, starting a business, writing a book; whatever your "IT" is, keep working, keep trying, keep pushing and keep going until you win!

STRENGTH ACTION PLAN: Identify your "IT" and start mapping out a plan to accomplish it, regardless of how long it takes. Make notes of your plan here:

_____

_____

_____

_____

_____

_____

_____

_____

_____

_____

_____

_____

_____

Day 10

DAY 10: Just Say No

I am learning in this journey called life that we cannot be all things to all people! I cannot tell you how many times I have overextended myself because I was afraid to just say, "No." I was afraid to hurt someone's feelings or disappoint someone at the expense of my own. Practicing self-care includes keeping it real and setting boundaries. There is only one art of saying no! One of my favorite slogans is *"Just Do It."* There is no other way to say no; you just must do it. The suggestion here is not for you to be mean or rude, but to clearly say no.

Imagine this scenario: you have been working hard all week long and you planned a day of rest on Saturday. You promised yourself after working five 12-hour days that you aren't going to lift a finger on Saturday, other than to sip on some ice-cold tea. Then a friend calls and asks if you can watch their child, pet, etc., so that they can go out on a date. You know that this good friend also deserves a break. What do you do? Do you sacrifice your time of relaxation? You must recognize what is in your best interest.

Identify the areas where it is prudent to say yes and those where you should simply just say no. Sometimes, when we say yes to help someone we are taking away an opportunity for them to learn and to grow. Sometimes you just do not have the time and space, physically or mentally! Learn the art of saying "No".

"You have to decide what your highest priorities are and have the courage pleasantly, smilingly, and non-apologetically – to say no to other things. And the way to do that is by having a bigger yes burning inside."

Stephen Covey

STRENGTH ACTION PLAN: Identify an area in your life where you can start exercising your right to say NO and how you will go about doing it. Make notes of your plan here:

_____

_____

_____

_____

_____

_____

_____

_____

_____

_____

_____

_____

Day 11

DAY 11: Keep It Real

Throughout my years on this earth (no I am not going to tell you how many years that is), many people have broken their promises to me. Those promises varied from, "I promise to stay true and be committed to you," "If there is anything you need let me know," "Call me anytime," "I'm here for you always..." The list goes on and on. I understand that people mean well. Their heart was in the right place and they intended to be there for me. However, the actions just did not line up with what they said or what they intended to do.

Be honest with yourself first, that you cannot be there for everyone when they need you to be. The reality is that we all have our own lives to live; we all have our own set of obstacles and challenges. So, let us start being true to ourselves and then to others by carefully being mindful of meaning what we say and following through and doing what we say.

Think carefully before you make a commitment or promise to someone. You never know how your lack of commitment and–follow-through can affect someone who is counting on you. Keep it real, be true to your word, and be a person people can count on that will follow through with your commitments and promises.

Now, if you are someone who has been disappointed by people, remember to be strong in the power of God's might, not defeated in the power of other people's weakness. People may not always be there as expected -- just like there are times that you have not been there for them. They may not be true to their words or promises but, God's promises are *"yea and...amen"* (2nd Corinthians 1:20). *"God is not a man that he shall lie..."* (Numbers 23:19) If He said it, then He is faithful and just to perform it! God is faithful to His Word.

STRENGTH ACTION PLAN: Identify an opportunity to allow God to be the source of your help and not people. Next identify an area in your life where you will start to do what you say you will do. Make notes of your plan here:

_____

_____

_____

_____

_____

_____

_____

_____

_____

_____

_____

Day 12

DAY 12: Positive Thoughts, Positive Words, Positive Changes

As a personal trainer, I know that we have the ability to shape our body. However, for true inner strength, we must work even harder to shape our minds. I tell my clients, "Where the mind goes, the body follows." I truly believe that if we think we can, WE CAN. The Bible declares, *"For as a man thinketh in his heart, so is he."* (Proverbs 23:7) It all starts with our thinking.

One of my clients who is 69 years old recently received a diagnosis of early-stage Parkinson's disease. A couple of weeks ago she came to train and was so down, and talking negatively. I told her how important it is to stay positive and to speak positively. Where the mind goes the body follows. We spent the entire session discussing the importance of practicing replacing negative thoughts with positive ones, then purposefully speaking the positive thoughts. Despite how we feel, we do not need to speak it out loud. We need to decree and declare good things over our lives – we have the power.

The next time she came in for a training session she had a different thought process and more positive words. She even stated that she noticed the difference in how she felt (although nothing changed physically) energy-wise. Purposeful thinking and speaking positively will bring about positive changes. She said, "I am not going to let this beat me!" I am so proud of her. She had a great session!

The Word of God declares in Proverbs 18:21 in the New International Version of the Bible (NIV) *"The tongue has the power of life and death, and those who love it will eat its fruit."* Think LIFE, Speak LIFE, Have LIFE!

STRENGTH ACTION: Identify a vision that you will WORK for - for yourself

without relying on someone else to do it for you. Make notes of your plan

here:

_____

_____

_____

_____

_____

_____

_____

_____

_____

_____

_____

_____

Day 13

DAY 13: Do Not Resist the Shift

Sometimes God will shift things to prepare us for His next move in our lives – a new opportunity that will catapult us to another level. The process may not feel good but it is necessary to get you ready. Stop looking shifts and changes as problems and look at them as a process to prepare you for something that you have been praying and believing for. He may unexpectedly move people out of your life. People are in your life for a reason and sometimes just a specific season.

Just like weather can change with the arrival of a new air mass. Ever notice how when it is about to snow that you can see a change in how the clouds look? You can almost smell cleaner air. How about when it is about to rain – do your joints start to ache? Some of us can predict the weather just by how our body feels. Ever notice how after the storm, how the crisp and clear the sky is and how beautiful it looks? Pay close attention to the signs that a shift is about to occur. After you get through the aches and pains there is something brighter and beautiful waiting for you just like the sky after the storm.

There are things you prayed for, and the path to the answer may not look like you think it should. Do not resist the shift and do not ignore the signs. God is preparing you for something better, bigger and greater. A shift may be necessary to prepare and position you properly – do not resist it, go with the flow of God's shift.

STRENGTH ACTION PLAN: Identify a shift that has been a challenge for you and consider how you can make it an opportunity to stand strong and grow. Make notes of your plan here:

_____

_____

_____

_____

_____

_____

_____

_____

_____

_____

_____

Day 14

DAY 14: Push Pass The Pain To Persevere

Every day I motivate, inspire and encourage others to be the best they can be despite my pain and my own need for the same encouragement. You may be thinking but, "you do not know what I have been through." You are right, I do not know. What I do know is everything that we go through in life it is up to us how we react to it. Charles Swindle said it best, *"...Life is 10% what happens to you and 90% how you react to it."*

It is essential to your growth to use every experience as an opportunity to pull yourself together and push your way through life's challenges – we all have them. You are not going to get stronger by singing somebody done me wrong song your whole life – get over it! Even if it is something so painful you cannot get over it, still push through the pain. At some point and time, you must decide – yes YOU! - That it is time to push on. If you never push, you will never give birth to the perseverance waiting on the other side of the pain. Just like a pregnant woman must push past the pain of childbirth, you too much push to give birth to your destiny. I am a firm believer that everything that we go through is for a purpose.

Consider the following poem in your perseverance to push pass the pain:

Pain

This pain is pushing me
Pushing me closer to my destiny

Helping me to give birth
To all my value and worth

This pain is pushing me
Pushing me closer to my destiny

Pain will no longer let me hide
All the good I have inside

Although a thorn in my flesh
This is only a test to bring out my best

This pain is pushing me
Pushing me closer to my destiny

~ Renee Dantzler

STRENGTH ACTION PLAN: Identify a painful experience you are going through right now, (or have carried from the past), that you can push through to find yourself on the side of perseverance. Make notes of your plan here:

_____

_____

_____

_____

_____

_____

_____

_____

_____

_____

_____

Day 15

DAY 15: Watch Your Inner Circle

The people who I thought were in my close circle in my time of grief have dwindled with time. Those who I thought were going to be part of my life-long support system have changed from one year to the next. It takes great inner strength to discern the people who are in your life for a reason and those who are there for just a season. I am more cognizant of time and the importance of redeeming the time we have, and I certainly do not want to waste time spending it with people who do not help, but are a hindrance to forward movement. The last thing you want is waste valuable time (a rare commodity) with people who are of no value to your life. Not everyone should have access to the inner sanctum of your life -- your heart. Your circle should encompass people who make you better, stronger, and wiser.

Take inventory of the people that are in your close inner circle. Think of yourself as a bank; take a moment to identify those who make deposits of strength, motivation, inspiration, and encouragement - leaving you fulfilled. These are positive influencers. Also, identify those individuals who only make withdrawals constantly withdrawing and leaving you empty, depleted and drained. These are the negative balancers and they must not be a part of your circle.

STRENGTH ACTION PLAN: Take inventory of anyone who you have allowed in your inner circle who is not making positive deposits into your life. Determine who can occupy that space -- and who cannot. Make notes of your plan here:

_____

_____

_____

_____

_____

_____

_____

_____

_____

_____

_____

_____

Day 16

DAY 16: Be A Source Of Strength

Do not mistake a moment of weakness for not being strong; we all have those moments. Only God is omnipotent! Strength is withstanding the many trials and storms of life. It is still getting up in the morning, still standing tall amid adversity, still believe God when it does not look like it is working out and still praying despite unanswered prayers. A strong individual can withstand great force and pressure and keep it moving.

I used to think that my ability to save face in front of my clients was just a mask. Thinking, am I being fake and not true to myself about how I felt on a given day? One of my mentors, Elder Nicole Mason said something so profound to me. She said, *"It is not a mask, it is God's fortifying power."* It is God who helps us to keep it together despite all the hell that might be going on in our lives. Do not get me wrong, we all cry sometimes. Crying is not a sign of weakness. It shows that you are human. The question now becomes, "Are you going to allow the emotion behind the tears to overtake you or take over you?"

When we allow God (who is the source of our strength) to help us hold our head up high and not let them see you sweat, then we become a source of strength to those around us.

STRENGTH ACTION PLAN: Think about areas of your life that you have overcome challenges. Identify how you can use that to be a source of strength to those around you. Make notes of your plan here:

_____

_____

_____

_____

_____

_____

_____

_____

_____

_____

_____

Day 17

DAY 17: Exercise Your Faith

There is nothing wrong with having high expectations; in fact, we should all set expectations for ourselves and others around us. However, you must marry those expectations with some actions. If you work for nothing that is exactly what you should expect. The Bible declares in James 2:26 *"Faith without works is dead..."*

Have you ever been the kind of person who expected a check in a mail, a knock at the door or a phone call that you just inherited some land or better yet, a billion dollars? Well if you do not go to the mailbox, or answer the door or phone, how do you expect to receive it?

Faith is a wonderful thing, believing in miracles and hoping for unexpected good things to happen but, without works, it is for naught. Get up and pray! Prayer is an action that helps to activate your faith. It unlocks many opportunities, blessings the Lord has in store. Exercise your faith and pray!

People who exercise their body expect something to happen. The expectations can vary from feeling good to losing weight, becoming faster, stronger and growing bigger muscles. That is not going to happen sitting on the couch. You must get up and move, walk, run, pull, push and lift something. As it is in the natural body, so it is with the spiritual. Think of Faith as a muscle that needs regular exercise to improve, grow, and get stronger. We all believe in something.

A simple act of sitting in a chair is faith. You trust and believe when you sit in a chair that it is going to hold you up. Start acting on your faith, do not just sit on the couch and wait. Put some action with it; apply for the job, buy that home, start a workout regimen, write that book. Do not delay, exercise your faith today!

STRENGTH ACTION PLAN: List areas in your life where you have faith, but no action. What actions can you take to exercise that faith? Make notes of your plan here:

_____

_____

_____

_____

_____

_____

_____

_____

_____

_____

_____

Day 18

DAY 18: Make A Change

"And the LORD God called unto Adam, and said unto him, where art thou?" (Genesis 3:9) God knew exactly where Adam was when He asked this question. The reality is, He is still asking this question today of many of us. I even have to ask *myself* every day, "Where am I in God?" "Where art thou?" Wait for an answer. If it is not where God would like you to be, then be strong, be courageous, look at the man in the mirror and make a change.

If you want to see change, you must make a change! You have heard it before - be the change you wish to see. Sadly, many people do not like change. We easily become comfortable with the familiar. I once heard a motivational speaker say, "There are only two people who like change and that is cashiers and babies." Change often takes us to unfamiliar territory which can be very uncomfortable. You must keep in mind, positive change is good.

Changing what you say is a good start. If you want to change the way you think, change the way you speak. The Bible declares in Proverbs 18:21 *"death and life are in the power of the tongue..."* The more we speak those things that be not as though they were, the more we create the change that we hope to see, and our thoughts begin to line up. Negative thoughts are inevitable, but we have the power, ability, and the right to stop those thoughts in its tracts. Your tongue is a powerful tool – use it wisely. Right smack in the middle of a negative thought, say, "Stop! No!" Change the line of thinking immediately. You have that power, just like that.

STRENGTH ACTION PLAN: Identify 3 areas in your life where making a change is necessary. Determine the steps to start implementing those changes until they are accomplished. Make notes of your plan here:

_____

_____

_____

_____

_____

_____

_____

_____

_____

_____

_____

_____

Day 19

DAY 19: Be Unique

God broke the mold when he made you. There is only one of you – no one is exactly like you. You are unique and have something to offer this world that no one else created to do. Do not try to be someone else and most importantly do not allow anyone to try to minimize the unique qualities that set you apart. I once heard someone say, *"You cannot be me because I am already taken."* I love that because it says to me that we are all original designs. We all have unique qualities that no one can duplicate, no matter how hard they try.

I am unapologetically me – be authentically and unapologetically you. Some people are going to like you; some are not. Some are going to appreciate you; some are not. Some people are going to love you; some are not. Some people understand you; some do not. The reality is, you are with YOU 24 hours a day/7 days a week and nobody else is. So be who you are, unapologetically. Do not try to fit in. In fact, unique is what is in and if it is not, no worries – just go ahead with your own version of uniqueness, and start a trend yourself!

Social media depicts images that can cause even the strongest of persons to question how they look and feel about themselves. Many of those images are either photoshopped or just not real. For those that are real, let us congratulate them and not try to duplicate. What is good for you is to take a look in the mirror and compete with that individual and no one else. Each day, you become a better version of your unique self!

STRENGTH ACTION PLAN: Identify something unique about you and list 3 ways to celebrate and harness it to become a better version of YOU! Make notes of your plan here:

_____

_____

_____

_____

_____

_____

_____

_____

_____

_____

_____

_____

Day 20

DAY 20: Set Goals

Many of us have dreams and aspirations in our head of what we would like to see happen in our lives. Ideas are great, but alone they are just good ideas. You must take it a step further by writing them down along with a plan of action.

When I was a corporate trainer, I had the privilege of teaching Time and Task Management to all the employees. The main objectives of the course were to explain to the participants how to better manage their day-to-day tasks and responsibilities productively. I trained the importance of creating a "To-Do List", how to systematically complete tasks and check each of them off the list. These tasks are markers or milestones to achieve a goal. When setting goals, the most common method is the SMART method. The premise for SMART goals is making the goals Specific, Measurable, Achievable, Realistic and Time Sensitive. This process is a great template for goal setting.

Do not let anybody tell you what you should do, what you can or cannot do. Just remember to set SMART goals using smaller milestones to reach your goals.

Do not expect anyone to work harder than you towards YOUR goals. I used to expect others to put forth just as much energy (if not more) to help me reach a goal. Then the thought came to me, "why should they?" It is YOUR goal, it is YOUR passion. It is up to you to put in the work and the energy for the vision.

Reality Check – When was the last time you felt more passionate about someone else's goal? Did your thoughts and sleep consume you with how you were going to put all of your time and energy into their goal or vision? Of course not! You see, no one will feel as passionate about YOUR goal as you do. It is up to YOU to put in the time for YOU.

STRENGTH ACTION PLAN: Write your goal(s) along with a plan of action using the SMART method. Make copies of this page for multiple goals.

Goal:
_____
_____
_____

Specific:
_____
_____

Measurable:
_____
_____

Achievable:
_____
_____

Realistic:
_____
_____

Time Sensitive:
_____
_____
_____

Day 21

DAY 21: Speak It Into Existence!

After losing my son, truthfully, I lost myself. I was not sleeping well, sometimes barely sleeping at all. My healthy eating habits were sporadic and sometimes just plain, bad. Quite frankly, there were moments when I just did not care and ate whatever I wanted.

My health and weight started spiraling out of control. As a personal trainer, I know what to do; exercise, eat a properly balanced diet, (food intake) and get proper rest, but none of that was working. I worked out five to six days a week. Sometimes, two times in one day but, my eating was not good. We have a saying in the fitness industry, you cannot out-train (exercise) a bad diet. I was allowing the ebbs and flows of the emotions of my grief to control me.

One day God spoke to my spirit and said, *"As a man thinketh in his heart, so is he."* (Proverbs 23:7). I had to start thinking differently and speaking differently regardless of how I felt. Speak health, speak wellness, and speak positively over yourself! That is what I began to do. I started speaking positive daily affirmations over my health and my wellness. "I eat well, I sleep well, I am well, I look well, I feel well, and all is well!"

Everything began to manifest slowly but surely. What area of your life do you need to apply this to? Begin to speak positively to and over yourself. Do not wait for someone else to do it. You have the power and control over your words. Remember, *"Death and life are in the power of the tongue..."* (Proverbs 18:21). Think Strong, Speak Strong, Live Strong, Be Strong!

STRENGTH ACTION PLAN: Identify areas in your life you have not spoken positively about, and determine how you can make a conscience and purposeful decision to start staying positive instead. Make notes of your plan here:

_____

_____

_____

_____

_____

_____

_____

_____

_____

_____

_____

_____

"Finally, my brethren, be strong in the Lord, and in the power of his might." Ephesians 6:10

In Loving Memory

In loving memory of my baby boy, Andrew (Drew); I know he wants me to be strong. So, in honor of him, I keep pushing, I keep pressing and I keep going.

Andrew's personality was one that lit up a room with his presence. His smile and energy made others around him feel better.

My prayer is that I do the same with my writing. I hope and pray that the words and energy from my writing will uplift and light up the lives of all who read it - much like Drew did with his friends and teammates.

I pray that I too, influence, impact, encourage, and inspire many people to be the strongest and best version of themselves.

JOURNEY STRONG

www.ingramcontent.com/pod-product-compliance
Lightning Source LLC
LaVergne TN
LVHW021540080426
835509LV00019B/2748